Published by

REARDON & SC
Publishers
56 Upper Norwood Street,
CHELTENHAM. GLOS. C

Written and Illustrated by
Mark Richards

ISBN 0 9508674 8 9

Revised Edition 1994

STOATE & BISHOP (PRINTERS) LTD
Shaftesbury Industrial Estate
The Runnings, Cheltenham, Glos.

Walks Around
STOW on the WOLD

by MARK RICHARDS

Reardon Publishing

River Dikler at Upper Swell

Stow-on-the-Wold

By virtue of its splendid location perched high upon the Cotswold ridge, at the junction of ancient trade routes, Stow-on-the-Wold has been, since its foundation by the monks of Evesham Abbey, a focus of North Cotswold rural life. Eight roads of varying present-day importance, radiate from Stow like the spokes of a wagon wheel. As a result visitors seeking to explore the immediate countryside can, if they are prepared to accept a modicum of road walking, swiftly discover the peace and joy of a genuine and richly rewarding Cotswold countryside.

Taken in its entirety the country walk covers eight undulating miles. However, link options make it possible to shorten the walk to meet personal time limitations. The principal options being:

A : Follow the main route to the Dikler footbridge just beyond Upper Swell crossing it to ascend the pasture to the stile and gate beside the lodge to Abbotswood, thereafter following the broad verged B4077 back to Stow — distance 6 miles.

B : Start by reversing the above option from Stow down the B4077 and the footpath to the footbridge. Then either complete the full walk via Hyde Mill — distance 5 miles, or ascend the B4068; beyond Pineapple Spa Cottage the verges become very narrow so caution is needed rising to the kissing gate left up steps. Cross the recreation ground, keeping to the north side of

3

the cricket pitch to enjoy the best of the north-west
-ward views. On reaching the metal gate into a
private road beside Talbot Square, enter Stow
Square by following the alleyway directly across
the Fosse Way — distance 3 miles.

C : The shortest circular walk from the Maugersbury
car park follows Park Street and Sheep Street
up to the Fosse Way junction. Keep on the
pavement (left) beside the Fosse Way down to
the old Maugersbury road turn left along the
main route — distance 1¾ miles.

D : Lastly, may I commend two simple backtracking
excursions. Either follow Well Lane down to
Broadwell to enjoy a stroll via the village green,
ford and streamside path to the church - the Fox
Inn is a welcome bonus for refreshment, before
retracing your steps — distance 3¾ miles.
Alternatively, reverse the last part of option B,
i.e. leave Stow Square through the alleyway at
the northern end (next to Grundy's), footpath sign
'Fosseway.' Cross the Fosse Way following the private
road ahead to the metal gate. Enter the recreation
ground, stroll down to the kissing gate at the bottom
and backtracking, the broad views justify the walk.

Profile showing the gradients on the walk

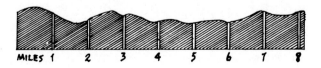

MILES 1   2   3   4   5   6   7   8

4

Approach to Stow Square from the free car park

Leave your car in the Maugersbury Park car park ascending Park Street, entering the narrow 'one way' Digbeth Street, right. Digbeth Street is an ancient thoroughfare marking the line of the Jurassic Way, the age old Cotswold Ridgeway. It is thought that the Jurassic Way ran the length of the Cotswold Hills from Bath stretching north to the Lincolnshire Wolds and terminating at the Humber estuary.

During the eleventh century whilst the manor of Maugesbury (pronounced *morg's-berry*), a sheep estate, belonged to Evesham Abbey, a lucrative market town was established in the angle between the Roman Fosse Way and the Cotswold Ridgeway. It was a time of expansion and rising wealth in the Cotswolds borne upon the 'Golden Age' of the wool trade (hence Sheep Street). Notice the Market Cross, only the lower portion is truly old, the gabled headstone, contemporary with the Victorian Town Hall, shows a rood on one face and the Abbot of Evesham recieving the market charter from Henry I on the other face. There are several handsome buildings facing the Square. St Edward's House (café) must be pre-eminent, boasting an early eighteenth century facade of fluted Corinthian pilasters. The parish church of St. Edward, on cruciform plan, deserves a visit, particularly when the tower is open to the public — as the highest point, in the highest town in the Cotswold (770 feet above sea level), it rivals Broadway Tower in the quality and extent of the panorama across hills and wood dappled vales.

The Walk begins ⸺

Leave the Square at its northern end along the High Street, into Parson's Corner road, leading right past Fosseway Farm Stables and Fosseway House, notice the church-like folly partially visible over the wall to the left. At the junction turn left (No Through Road) down Well Lane pass Stow Well, a popular resort to idle away a sunny day, the cool clear resurgence splashes into a large stone trough.

Pass Top Lodge, enter the confined pathway, with views opening southwards to Adlestrop Hill and the distant Wychwood Forest horizon, ⟁ leading straight down to the Broadwell road. Continue downhill into the village. You may like to walk across the Green to inspect the ford and huge memorial stone to Lord Ashton of Hyde.

Follow the stream back onto the road by the Fox Inn (excellent bar food and real ale). The attractive inn-sign features a fox overlooking Donnington Brewery (passed a little later in the walk) and on the other side a fox slyly hiding from a huntsman under a bank.

Advance with the road branching right upon the delightful streamside path. At the top go left from the bus shelter along the road (notice the pool of the 'broad well' over the wall to the right). At the sharp corner take the footpath signposted right, negotiate the narrow gateway, and the muddy ground beyond, to a new hunting gate (please shut gate, notice). Ascend the paddock to a second hunting gate, glancing left to admire the Georgian-styled Manor House, built in

1757 in golden ashlar. Pass through the churchyard via the kissing gates. The church, St. Paul's (guide to parish and church on sale within) boasts a beautiful tympanum (which is the space between the lintel of the doorway and the arch above it), carved with a Maltese Cross reset from a former Norman doorway over the narrow door on the north side of the tower and Saxon carved stones in the porch. Reaching the road, via the handrailed steps, go right

St. Paul's

and left at the road junction, signposted 'Donnington.' **2** Cross the Fosse Way (wary of speeding traffic). Linking Axminster with Lincoln this Roman Road was created as the first military frontier and supply line for the control of Brittania. The name 'fosse' being handed down from the Latin for 'ditch', no doubt a reference to the dykes that flanked this 'strata via' (straight way). On the bare space to the right of the Donnington road stood, until eight years ago, a farm cottage.

7

Stow-on-the-Wold probably derives its name from 'the holy place on the bare hill.' The earliest reference to the settlement being circa 1107 'Edwardstowe.'

St. Edward's Well rises quite distant from the hill-top settlement at the foot of South Hill, overgrown and forgotten. Unlike the popular rendezvous of Stow Wells situated in Well Lane which command a splendid view eastward across the Evenlode Vale to the wooded ridge above Adlestrop.

WALKS around STOW ·ON·THE· WOLD

KEY

S : STILE
K : KISSING GATE
g : BRIDLE GATE
G : FIELD GATE

TROUT FARM ¼

mill pond

Donnington Brewery

Manor House

Upper Swell

Long Barrow

Old Farmhouse Hotel

Lady's Well

Lower Swell

tel.

Golden Ball

Primary School

Rectory Farm

Bow

Pine Cott

grass verge

River Dikler

Nether Swe Manor

Hyde Mill

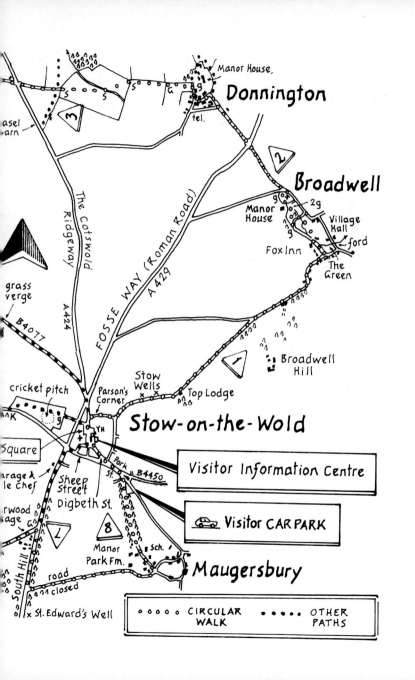

Manor House.

Donnington

tel.

3

asel
arn

2

Broadwell

Manor
House

9 2g

9

Village
Hall

Fox Inn

ford

The
Green

grass
verge

B4077

A 424

THE CATSWOLD RIDGEWAY

FOSSE WAY (Roman Road) A 429

1

Broadwell
Hill

Stow
Wells

cricket pitch

Parson's
Corner

Top Lodge

K

9

Stow-on-the-Wold

YH

Square

Park
St.

B4450

arage &
le Chef

Sheep
street

Digbeth St.

rwood
age

7

8

Visitor Information Centre

🚗 **Visitor CAR PARK**

Manor
Park Fm.

Sch.

Maugersbury

South Hill

road
closed

x St. Edward's Well

○ ○ ○ ○ ○ CIRCULAR
WALK

● ● ● ● OTHER
PATHS

Proceed towards the shy hamlet of Donnington, admiring the views right towards Brailes Hill and Ilmington Downs. The earliest reference to Donnington dates from 779 A.D. 'Dunnestreatun' which describes the boundary of 'Dunna's farm' defined by the Fosse Way.

Take the righthand fork in the road, following it round the sharp lefthand bend at the entrance to the eighteenth century Manor House, climbing into the tiny community. At the top turn right, along the lane to a metal gate on the left, just beyond the old hand water-pump. Walk diagonally right, beyond the row of elm stumps, to the metal field gate. Thereafter, follow the track beside the hedge to a stile beside a gateway. Descend the bank just below the earth landslip, a continuous process, caused by a spring undermining the load of soil. Aim for the first ash tree in the valley bottom where cross the rail-sleeper bridge and stile. Go right, gently rising over the ridge and furrow pasture (noticably more lush than the opposing pasture, which is devoid of ridge and furrow); en route to the stile look right to locate Banks Fee House c.1760 and the village of Longborough. **3** Entering a short lane advance onto the Broadway road. Show due caution in crossing the A424. Notice the handsome cavalier-like relief inside the pediment of the house facing the junction.

Follow the unclassified road signed 'Condicote and Trout Farm'. A road enters to the right from the A424, a short way up this road is Town Quarry, where quarrying ceased upon the discovery of rich deposits of dinosaur bones; the most recent Cotswold finds feature the world's earliest Stegosaurus (at Stonesfield, Oxford).

10

Continue, taking the road signed 'Upper Swell' left, which leads into the Dikler valley. Pass Arkell's Brewery (no public access), the picturesque home of Donnington Ales for 120 years, complete with a large mill pond with islands the happy resort of a multitude of ducks. The Arkell family are linked through marriage with the late Sir Peter Scott, hence the wild fowl. Follow the minor road into the valley bottom crossing the river Dikler, this appealing river-name derives from the Saxon meaning 'place thick with rushes'; a tributary of the river Windrush which itself ironically has nothing whatsoever to do with rushes in its origins (though corrupted to appear so), being an even more ancient British name.

4 The narrow road rises to meet the Tewkesbury road (B4077). Go left into the tiny village of Upper Swell (without the highway what a beautiful spot this would be - a scene that inspired Claude Monet, the nineteenth-century French impressionist painter to commit to canvas). Notice the deft way the present owners of the Manor have adapted the half stone-built dutch barn into a landscaping of the former farmyard as an ornamental garden.

With due caution slip round the blind bend in the road. Visit the charmingly simple Norman parish church of St. Mary adjacent to the early seventeenth-century Manor House, with its fine two storey Jacobean ashlar porch. Lower down the road the nineteenth-century mill still retains its wheel (though no longer operative). Notice too, the quite beautiful eighteenth-century road bridge robustly coping with modern traffic.

Take the footpath signed 'Lower Swell', the hunting gate is swiftly succeeded by a stile to inhibit illegal horse traffic: why the prominent notice refers to horses at all is something of a mystery, as too the need for the fenced passage running along the foot of the paddocks (no legal right-of-way), as mounted horses could not process!

The footpath crosses the fence stile, ascending half right, via a mid-course fence stile, to a stile near the top corner (alternatively you may follow the fenced passage for an intimate view of the Dikler, striking uphill from the single-parapeted stone footbridge to reach the kissing gate). Advance to a second kissing gate where notice left the overgrown funnelled access to a stock drinking place in the river Dikler.

The footpath advances upon a shallow bank to a third kissing gate in the metal fence and beyond reaches a fourth kissing gate onto the private road to Abbotswood (house). **5** Go right, past Bowl Farm, notice (right) the novel dairy building modified from a seventeenth century dovecote. This dates from the time when Sir Robert Atkyns was Lord of the Manor — he was the author of the classic topographical study of 1776 'The Ancient and Present State of Gloucestershire.' The initials 'M.F.' over the lintel at Bowl Farm, which occur on numerous Swell cottages refer to Mark Fenwick, for whom Sir Edwin Lutyens designed Abbotswood in 1902. The pre-eminent architect of his time, both in Britain and the Commonwealth, Abbotswood represents Lutyen's most important Cotswold work.

Following the drive towards the lodge notice, on the left, the humble stone conduit known as Lady's Well. On reaching the road make a brief diversion left, ascending the pavement to inspect Pineapple Spa Cottage. It was built in 1807 when a mineral spring was discovered, hence the plaque over the lower doorway stating 'carbonated chalybeate'. Architecturally very Indian like, Sezincote being the vogue model, the projected Spa resort failed to materialise; the spring still flows but is sealed beneath the cottage floor.

Pineapple Spa Cottage

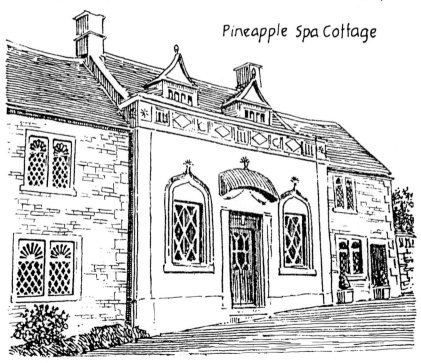

Enter Lower Swell beside the B4068. The origin of the unusual village-name Swell is thought to mean 'settlement on a low ridge' as in 'swell' of land. Take the bridle lane, signposted from the Golden Ball, leading through Rectory Farm to the village street opposite the primary school. Go left, bearing left down the bridle lane (No Through Road sign) passing Ferndale House to a gate. The bridleway proceeds to a gateway before descending near the wood to a gate. **6** Then through a short passage beside a fenced-off marshy depression and on to a gate and sleeper bridge over a tributary of the river Dikler. The bridleway continues via a further gate next to an odd shed set upon a pool, then to a gate into the lane adjacent to Hyde Mill Farm.

Go left crossing the broad sleeper bridge over Dikler (mill pond), take a left turn through the gate (signed 'Stow-on-the-Wold'). Cross the ridge and furrow pasture, notice the stretched 'S' alignment, evidence that these old cultivation ridges were the product of oxen ploughing. Pass to the left of the piggery to a stile, follow the track uphill (watch the waymarking) via a series of gates passing stables and cross the approach drive to Nether Swell Manor. The footpath continues more steeply via a series of white gates beside stabling to reach a bridle gate into the scarp woodland. Slant right up to a stile, thereafter crossing the pasture rising to a stile/gate (to the right of a copse). Be sure to take a backwards glance, the spacious westward views range across the limestone wolds towards Broadway Tower.

The walk enters a lane, passing a farm and cottages to reach the Fosse Way. The walk may be terminated by crossing (with the utmost caution) the Fosse and following the tarmac path left into Stow.

7 The more agreeable conclusion is to go right downhill The freak storm of 27 March 1990 wrought havoc to many of the mature gangly beeches flanking the Fosse Way here on South Hill. The road was blocked for several days and left an unsightly mess of skyward roots and shattered drystone walls.

Go left along the Maugersbury road, the posts at the beginning effectively closing vehicular access onto the busy A429. The views are now of Icomb Hill and the Evenlode valley, last seen above Donnington. Entering Maugersbury turn left immediately after passing the No Through Road sign, ascend the minor road to pass through the old park gates into the Maugersbury Park Avenue, sometimes called Tunnel Lane, **8** to finish the grand circular walk.

Donnington Brewery

15

LOOK Out!
for our other products

The Donnington Way
Cotswold River Walks
Walks Around Chipping Norton
Cotswold Driveabout - The Northern Cotswolds
Cotswold Driveabout - The Southern Cotswolds
Cotswold Walkabout
Cotswold Hillwalks
Gloucestershire Walkabout
The Echo's Cotswold Walks
The Haunted Cotswolds
Plus various others available throughout the Cotswolds
and nearby Counties

REARDON & SON
Publishers

56 Upper Norwood Street
Leckhampton
Cheltenham Glos GL53 0DU

Phone 231800
STD 0242

Whilst every care has been taken to ensure the accuracy of this book, neither the author or publishers hold themselves responsible for any errors that may be found, or for the reader's interpretation of the text or illustrations.